Vantage thoughts

Thivya Jayakumar

BookLeaf Publishing

India | USA | UK

Presentation by *BookLeaf Publishing*

Web: www.bookleafpub.com

E-mail: info@bookleafpub.com

ISBN: 978-93-94788-01-5

First edition 2022

PREFACE

Before you begin this collection of Ballads, I would like to acknowledge something,

In my quest for reading human minds, I realised every life is unique and every human deserves and desires in one's own unique way. But, as nature is mysteric there is something common among everyone's life - LOVE and HATE.

My book is intended to describe life with some examples that I came across and acquired which I hope depicts atleast of part of human thoughts and reactions at their happiest or worst moments and the way I adore it.

Life – Boon and Rune

Years rolled by,
She and her entire cohort are eligible to vote…
Still, he treats her as a tot.
He holds her hands to cross the lane,
and loves to play with her brownish mane.
Seasons changed as days passed but not her
habit to hold his hands on sleep...

The courage he gave to jump horizons,
The cordial thoughts he showed on her interests,
At times, raised a silent envy even among her
peers!

Every footstep and every crazy act of happiness
Had one thing in common – resilient love and
laughter.
He didn't fulfill all her cravings
He just gave the virtues to create her paving.

To him, raising a lass was not just a matter of
pride
And her attitude to decode runes crossed all tide

To the world he was just a tiring farmer…
But to her he was an unsung angel and she
called him, "dad!"

Blue Skies

Someone who never stopped being mischievous,
has now started to be polite and courteous.
Someone who leaped out of home every day to
play,
is now reckoned by time and place to decide her
virtues…
Someone who cried out even for bloodshed in
movies
Is now ready to face and fight every obstacle on
her own.
Someone who believed fantasy and luck from
childhood,
Is now striving hard to fulfil her own desires.

Love, life and destiny – obscure seeds that we
know not what they yield,
Still wish to get the best cherry of all from the
woods.
Time not just changes people but also
perspectives.
Mellowing from a naughty tyke to a tidy
woman…

Being "her" who is always deemed to behave
matured may be the reality

Still the kid having "blue skies" within her is
bliss!

Love Unrequited

"Why doesn't she turn around…
I couldn't gaze her seductive smile!",
he moaned at the last bench.
Two things that he is madly obsessed of…
is his guitar strings and her quirky winks
Every insane expression of her made up his art
gallery.
The day she entered the corridor in a red garb,
He blushed and adorned his shirt the whole day,
Such unplanned dress codes were always
beautiful!

She was the only song that he was unable to
narrate in his chords.
He was a bold, funny and talkative lad
but every time they met… his brain stumbled to
frame words
in her mesmeric charm!
Like a daily tramp following its track,
Walking back home, he strolled behind her
footsteps.

Not just looks but her attitude to handle
unpleasant situations
marked her first impression in his thoughts.

No teasing from his friends bothered him…
when staring her winsome presence.

Little she did know her presence mattered,
And every step of him was perfectly noted…
Still, she pretended to be ignorant of this
unrequited fondness!

Riddled

Trying to solve a simple riddle,
Cleared some long-term queries in middle.
A five-letter word…
That could make rivals as brothers,
Solve brawls, vanish egos, build trust
And make world a better place to live!

That's the most difficult stunt to perform before enemies,
And something one could not fake for a long time.
It may not be the answer to all the questions of life
Still, it simplifies the quest.

Finally found the most simple secretive answer,
"S-m-i-l-e" … the riddle resolved, and I
continued to follow the solution for life.

No matter how long the journey is,
Spread the fragrance of kindness
Smile with no grudge
And end up the jaunt with no person to live the way,
we lived a day!

Amour

Friendship and love both never comes on plan,
It just happens and that's it!
To last long or to suffer is the choice
Until then it's our time to rejoice.

Trust me no one agrees he is that attractive,
unless they know him by heart!
The moments when he pursued me in silence
I thought it all just as lust and appetence.

But even after years the yearning to see him...
The moments that are still fresh, the day when I
first saw him.
The way I stared at him when he stopped gazing
me,
The times his absence in-turn meant boring
routines!
Even phonetics fails to explain my heartbeat
When he crossed me accidentally.
I called it to be an unnamed affection
And my friends teased it be so called "love"

It was a satire fondness that we never expressed
Reliving some blissful memories of teen

I discern my feelings for him are not just mean
Love and pain can never be phrased to its fullest
by words
Both could be just felt or ignored.

Someday and somehow my anxious heart still
has a hope
to confess my "unnamed amour"!

Ecstasy Redefined

Sometimes life is hard
But most of the time we assume it so!
Each one of us have these people in our lives…
Who treated us like precious pearls on one day,
and worn out scrap the next day,
when we needed them the most
Still, we love them with millions of reasons to
hate!

Everything between them was so casual,
That they didn't realize their destiny was
together
and no one had to confess it either!
And now no one she had to cry out her agony.

She was shattered into pieces,
When she saw "him" after years...
and he just disdained her presence!
The glimpse of someone whom she yearned for
a long time
Has now not even recognized her mien.
She didn't have the courage to stop his way,
Nor forget his ignorance as they say.

Sometimes letting go,

Is the highest form of love we can show.
Let it return…if we our destiny is inexorable!
Until then it's her turn to stop her mind
from hallucinating his presence beside.
"Love is an overrated ecstasy", she sighed!

Never to Forever

"Pets look into your eyes and blink slowly
Trying to convey they love you, more than what
you do",
As he read through the lines,
His memory recaptured a flash of her dreamy
eyes!
Though reluctant to speak and felt shy,
he knew she always looked in his eyes when
away, like a spy!

 Still now all he dithers for…
Is to choose between his desires and
commitments.
Switching between destiny and choices,
All he dreamt of was a destiny of his choice.
When he met the dreamy eyes after years, he
was not out of words
But out of promises and hope!

Life is solely independent,
Still, we need that someone to be complete.
At times, we don't get to choose the right
person…
and other times right people don't meet at right
places!

The boon of love is,
It is not easy to be someone's "forever"!
And he longed for that moment to stand before
her,
Hold her slender hands and confess that - she is
his "Forever".

Love and Hope

Most blissful things of life… "Love and wind"
Both capable of reviving smile,
When smooth they bring heaven on earth
But at tough times both could blow away the
entire mirth!

Every time it's not about the promise
It is all about keeping it alive!
In general, promises mean declaration
But, for some all it means is "hope"!
And ultimately hope denotes love.

If artists could paint love
It would be the most beautiful portrait ever!
If love and hope could be explained in words,
They would have been just words for years.

From a love and hope statistics taken,
There are three moirae of life…
'What you want,
What you deserve
Changing want to desire.'
And we all know life is gifted when we reach
the third!

A Letter from Him

" 'You' made me speechless,
and my heart breathless
not just on the first glimpse but on every sight!
My thoughts got struck up like a frozen brook
and hands shivered as that of a senescent human,
when we started to chat and roam around.
Messages and emojis made our day,
and I always wanted you to stay.

I know you are a logophile...
Still, I am out of words to describe my craze for
you.
I had fumbled almost all precious moments of
my life...
But adoring you is the most beautiful mistake of
my soul!

I had never spelled out the fondness on you,
even when I thought to...
On the days when we had a walk through the
autumn fall, the way home.
At the moments when we shared that hesitant
eye contact,

the minutes when I just kept gazing at you and
did nothing.
Even poets would struggle for metaphors
to describe the beauty of your kind heart!

I know there were millions of chances to confess
this,
and I had spoiled or missed each on my own.
And hoping it' s not too late to utter this...
…..
"Sorry" for making this hard
and "Love you" for everything to cope with this
mad! "
Her eyes melted down with tears,
lips with pleasant smile...
as she completed reading the letter from him.
Alarmed by the sounds of her doorbell...
he just stood there blushing and smiling at his
own shyness
to confess this on his knees!

Inseparable

Someone said love is in the air
and she was lucky to find it's source now!
Fights, gossips, heart breaks...
nothing made then apart.

Teasing her was his full time job,
At times, she even tempted to sob
but some bonds are irreplaceable,
as they knew he was her tom and she was his
jerry.

He was a grown up kid,
She was a wavering kite in his hands
He was happy to hover around with her
and she was glad to be tied to his amour.
He was her shore,
wherever she wavered, she was destined to him!

Admiring the beauty of his anger
Losing himself in her pleasing sorry,
Every fight had it's own reason of love!
Being together not just means care and ponder
upon,
It is being at liberty and that is what love relies
on.

Perfect couple doesn't exist...
love lies in those imperfections
and beauty lies in rectifying them!

Squabbles of love

A poetry needn't be large and tangled
It could be like her... short, sweet and simple.
Meaning of it shouldn't be dumb
It should be like him... lank and lovely!
making a winsome pair.

He counted stars every time he gets mad
to calm the storm inside
And this time he counted one more from earth,
leaving those on the sky aside...
when she hugged him tight after a fight!

Every fight had two things in common,
finding faults on each other
and at the end sitting together
to resolve the hassles of love!

"Alright let's sort this out together"
makes life beautiful
that millions of surprises and love quotes!

If beauty is defined by love and care
then she was the beauty queen
and he was the most handsome man,

people could ever know.
More the squabbles, most enjoyable their fights
were!

Be You

If you are happy; laugh out
If you are angry; blow out
If you are lonely; join a mess
If you are doubtful; just guess!

If you are princess, feel happy to lend
If you are a cobbler, feel happy to mend

Millions of "ifs" and just one chance to traverse.
Being alive doesn't mean...
We are living our life.
The better part of life is to give,
The best part of life is to live!
Let's be the horizon to someone's darkness
or just a backbench to someone's tiredness.

Some thing that humans are easy at is to just
blame
Not all joy comes from that fame!
Accept faults, appreciate enemies
Find joy in every tiny spot of the travel.
Never be the audience of your own game.

If someone could portray the best of you... it's
you!

Magic

Sometimes an alarming nightmare
turns into a pleasant boon,
Exchanging rings didn't clear fears
His attitude to break taboos did!

The way he handled her
is the way she preferred to handle life,
troubles with smile and muddles with love!

It is easy to make someone laugh
but hard to keep them happy.
Every time she gets mad,
he bribed her anger with his smile!

Someone asked the superlative of love,
and she coined a new term with his "name".

He was a brainy programmer
but she was the best at decoding
the fret lines on his head,
when stress burns his day.

Happy or sad;
Blank or emotional,
he was her storyteller

and she was his magician
both dissolved pains and condensed love!

The New Beginning

It was her first time to have this flair inside,
The way she was excited looked insane...
Adoring her to be muse he spent everyday in
vain
From the day she found the two red lines on her
kit,
the more he had one more version of her to love,
the instance when he started to preach her how
to walk,
everything changed... even her simple life was
ready to accept pains!

They were delighted for a better new beginning
which they could make it best
For someone special who could give the truly
define
all the love and care they shared until then.
For someone who could bring glee
on every second even at their worst!

He was ready to persuade even gods
to relax her pains and eliminate the odds
She was ready to conquer world for him
with her umbilical support now!

Love from Nonage

He was jealous of every wave that hit up the
shore,
As it was privileged to play with her more
Even her pets had to stay out of sight,
on his every possessive fight!

She always dreamt of a little version of him
But this "he" was out of her syllabus.
The little tot had a lot to convey,
Lot more to explore and tots of questions to
annoy her!
Still being a budding foster...
she learnt every possible way to convince him.

Being a "mom" was difficult at home,
but being "dad" was tough everywhere!
He had to behave smart though he was not,
and tirelessly google brattish queries a lot.

Someone asked "is the baby fine?"
They just thought all their efforts to answer are
in vain.
Being first friends of every child on earth,
Rather than making sacrifices

the couple now on had to empathize the child's
desires!

Spending time together with the little brat,
they knew the real synonym of "Care".

Catastrophe

At times, our heart feels heavy even at the
happiest moments,
She felt that every time,
When she laughed out loud
When she celebrated gatherings with glee in
crowd,
When her adorning son hugged her on every
wake
when her hubby kissed her forehead on every
walk!

Being happy was always her passion
Still smile on her lips was under auction
Somedays she owned it ; other days she ruined
it!
She knew she could change nothing
but only get pacified that she was breathing.

From the moment she was diagnosed with a
malignant tumor
she didn't have the courage to accept anymore
amour
Her heart didn't wish to disclose the threat
 and her mind didn't want to hide it!

Sleepless nights, clouded thoughts
with hopeless smiles filled her days;
and her only rejoice was her cheerful family!

First Love

"May be florals define the beauty of nature
still no bud to flower bloomed ever on earth
could match the fragrance of my mother's
apparel"
His eyes flooded in tears as he re-read his first
lines to his first love!
Since, his heart broke and reality shook now,
on the day he knew his mom was incurably ill.

She wasn't that brilliant,
but she taught him every value to become a
human!
and the world name her "Mom".
Obsessing himself with her smile on his every
success;
he couldn't accept the fact that nothing is
permanent.

She was that person every kid needs in life,
someone to stay back and guide,
someone to watch us fall and rise;
and to teach what is wise.
Some days to err and learn,
Foster to have dreams of one's own,

and be proud and glad of one's success than
oneself!
She was a real begetter and a wonderful human
whose lap he longed to lie down now!

Nothing is more agonizing,
than a young man's cry in silence...
and helplessness to throw death away from his
"first love"!

Far off rainbow

Breaking through the toughest tussles of life,
all she longed for was serenity without strife.
Someone said god troubles the good-hearted
and so she doubted why he choose her!
Little she knew...
if someone who could ache more than herself for
her blight,
was her family and thus realised that god was
right!

Unlike other dramatic cryfests,
she didn't list leaving her family as a sob reason
but rather had courage to accept her fear of
death!
She packed the groceries with name tags,
wrote down all her secure lock passwords,
jotted down the details that she kept safe so far
and completed spinning her so called last
woolen scarf for her son.

The family knew their silent cries are in vain
and so made her smile at any cost even in pain.
Sitting under the winter rains at night,
now all she wished for, was a rainbow of hope to
fight;

not the death but the conflict of thoughts that her
mind thinks!
But as everyone said she was the strongest of the
kindred,
and so nothing could stop her not even death,
from caring and completing her daily chores.

May be guessing the end of an unknown journey
is easy
but, knowing the end of life and surviving is not!

The last Aurora

It was a pleasant breezy morning,
with birds chirping the entire lawn,
as his heart got a better hope in the dawn;
Everything seemed to be warm and poise,
until the moment she called his name in her
fading voice!

The calmness of the day suddenly turned into an
agitated mozart,
as she held his hands tight in pain for support.
The father and son released the most precious
gem they possessed,
is now under auction and they are out of bucks
to retain the glory!

Still managed to spell her irrelevant thoughts
before she forgets in pace,
and kissed her son's forehead trying hard to
remember his face.
She knew her memories are out of sight to fall
back and cry
and so the last few seconds of her life cannot
replay anything but just die!

Tears whelmed his eyes at the sight of her dulcet
smile...
He found it rains in moon too... when she cried
in serenity!
Silence prevailed, not even the birds chirped for
a while,
and she broke it this time...
"I am proud to be your's!" were her last words...
Holdingn his hands, she let her soul fly!

A Note to Heaven

"Her smile made an art on my ashes,
Her presence surrounded me with warmth,
She was that change that life wanted me to
acquire.
What more you need when you lose every hope
in life
Still, feel being broken is not always bad
Since you have a hope better than divinity
beside!

The way she took care of my comfort,
The way she taught what life is,
the way she smiled at my angry face,
The way she handled my mood swings,
Every thought of her makes me fall more and
more
for her heart of sheer love!

There were moments when we were delighted to
grow old together
and now why didn't she wait for her greys to
beautify our life farther!
May be I am not lucky though
to adorn her wrinkled curves.

I am waiting for nothing here but for her,
Since the only memory that her alzeimer's didn't
take away...was my name!
If alphabets are to be rearranged by amour,
Let "U" and "I" be together forever atleast
then..."

He smirked and ended his 50th anniversary note
at her grave!

Promise

Everytime it is not about the promise made,
It's all about keeping it alive!
Even after years of her demise,
his memory didn't refrain to relive her
memories.
Sometimes on aging in a state of trance,
At times, he starts analysing his purpose to live,
the glipmse of her face flashed and he got a
reason to strive.
He knew he may not be able to dream her
presence if her leaves earth
and so planned to stay to the fullest and rejoice
his birth!

Something that he found beautiful about himself
was,
his name in her voice...
and it kept echoing in every vein of him!

Silence in sorrow is mere acceptance
but smile in havoc is the real serenity!
And she was the perfect example of a serene
soul
who accepted death way before it reached her
bowl.

Being a part of her , nothing could decent his
strong faith and stronger memory.

He lied down under her feet smiling with tears
 as her grave read the way she decided years
ago,
"No one could define love and life better than
my dear did!"
And he closed his eyes gazing her grave to meet
her at heaven.